D0776408

Always Remember How Special You Are to Me

Blue Mountain Arts®

New and Best-Selling Titles

By Susan Polis Schutz:
To My Daughter with Love on the Important Things in Life
To My Son with Love

By Douglas Pagels:
Always Remember How Special You Are to Me
Required Reading for All Teenagers
The Next Chapter of Your Life
You Are One Amazing Lady

By Marci:
Angels Are Everywhere!
Friends Are Forever
10 Simple Things to Remember
To My Daughter
To My Granddaughter
To My Mother
To My Son
You Are My "Once in a Lifetime"

By Wally Amos, with Stu Glauberman:
The Path to Success Is Paved with Positive Thinking

By Minx Boren:
Friendship Is a Journey
Healing Is a Journey

By Carol Wiseman:
Emerging from the Heartache of Loss

Anthologies:
A Daybook of Positive Thinking
A Son Is Life's Greatest Gift
Dream Big, Stay Positive, and Believe in Yourself
Girlfriends Are the Best Friends of All
God Is Always Watching Over You
The Love Between a Mother and Daughter Is Forever
Nothing Fills the Heart with Joy like a Grandson
There Is Nothing Sweeter in Life Than a Granddaughter
There Is So Much to Love About You... Daughter
Think Positive Thoughts Every Day
Words Every Woman Should Remember
You Are Stronger Than You Know

Always Remember How Special You Are to Me

Words of appreciation for a truly wonderful person

Douglas Pagels

Blue Mountain Press™
Boulder, Colorado

Copyright © 2016 by Blue Mountain Arts, Inc.

All rights reserved. No part of this publication may be reproduced, stored in a retrieval system or transmitted in any form or by any means, electronic, mechanical, photocopying, recording or otherwise, without the written permission of the publisher.

Library of Congress Control Number: 2015959325
ISBN: 978-1-59842-982-4

◪ and Blue Mountain Press are registered in U.S. Patent and Trademark Office.
Certain trademarks are used under license.

Printed in China.
First Printing: 2016

♻ This book is printed on recycled paper.

This book is printed on paper that has been specially produced to be acid free (neutral pH) and contains no groundwood or unbleached pulp. It conforms with the requirements of the American National Standards Institute, Inc., so as to ensure that this book will last and be enjoyed by future generations.

Blue Mountain Arts, Inc.
P.O. Box 4549, Boulder, Colorado 80306

In all the days ahead, whenever you see this book, I want you to think of me and remember… all these special things about you.

After you read this book, I want you to set it aside and remember it when you're feeling happy and thankful, so you can remind yourself that... that's how you make me feel...

I hope you will put this someplace where you'll see it when you need a little cheering up, so you will remember that I'll always be here to help chase any clouds away.

There is never a day when you're not in my thoughts. And so many of the smiles in my heart are there... because of you.

I want you to remember that every time you see this book sitting on a shelf... and in all the days to come. You are one of the most special people in all the world to me.

And you always will be.

Do You Know How Important You Are to Me?

I know you probably wonder from time to time what you mean to me.
So I'd like to share this thought with you, to tell you that you mean so much to me.

Think of something you couldn't live without... and multiply it by a hundred.

Think of what happiness means to you... and add it to the feeling you get on the best days you've ever had.

Add up all your best feelings and take away all the rest… and what you're left with is exactly how I feel about you.

You matter more to me than you can imagine and much more than I'll ever be able to explain.

I want you to know that you're one amazing person.

You are so good to the people in your life. So considerate and caring. When you give, it's easy to see that it comes straight from the heart... and it gives everyone around you the gift of a nicer world to live in.

I love how strong you are inside. I always see that quality shine in you, and it reassures me to know — even though you face hardships and uncertainties just like many people do — there's a way through and a brighter day ahead. You're my reminder to be a little more brave, to not be so afraid, and to remember that things will turn out okay in the long run...

I love the way you don't let the crazy, difficult days get you down. I admire your ability to put things in perspective. To laugh when you can. To cry when you must. But always to try and make things better.

I hope you'll never forget how much I treasure just being in this world with you. And I love knowing that everyone else feels the same way I do. To your friends, you are everything a friend should be. To your family, I know you are dearly loved and truly the best.

You are such a deserving person. And I really hope that all of your days are as beautiful and as bright... as the ones you inspire in other people's lives.

Not all angels have wings.

But they're angels… all the same.

You can tell them from the way they light up the day, the hugs they give, and the way they bless other people's lives with so much abundance.

You are an every-day-angel to me, a truly beautiful one, and I don't know what I'd ever do without you.

I am beyond lucky to have you in my life.

I don't have all the words to express how important you are to me. Some words just don't go deep enough. But I want to say a very special thanks... all the same.

Within my heart is a place that is filled with warm and endearing feelings... feelings that understand how seldom someone like you comes along.

May You Be Blessed with All These Things

A little more joy,
a little less stress,
a lot more recognition of
your wonderfulness.

Abundance in your life,
blessings in your days,
dreams that come true,
and hopes that stay.

A rainbow on the horizon,
an angel by your side...
and everything
that could ever bring
a smile to your life.

You are so great. You're an inspiration to me... and to everyone who knows you.

Everything you do is done in the spirit of sharing and caring and making your corner of the world a better one. When people think of you, they think of a helping hand, a loving heart, and one of the sweetest people on the planet.

I am in awe of your strength, your gentleness, and all the blessings you bring to the people who are fortunate enough to be in your life.

You sacrifice and support and give so much of yourself. And I have to imagine that if you're sometimes a little tired at the end of the day, it's only because you have gone so far out of your way to make life nicer for everyone else.

You have so many qualities that just sparkle inside you! You meet every description of what I've always imagined a remarkable person would be. Your heart is so big and you're so good at sharing smiles wherever you go.

You can make my whole day just by saying something that only you could say... in that very caring, completely natural, sometimes serious, often funny, and always precious way.

Your presence — in person — is a delight. And your voice on the phone is the best medicine anyone ever invented.

You are a gift that makes me happy beyond words, makes everything just shine, and makes me feel so good.

It is a joy to have you so sweetly in my days and so dearly in my heart.

Especially for You

I may not always have the perfect words to tell you this, but I want you to know that I am so glad I have you in my life.

It's hard for me to decide what I like most about you. There are so many things to choose from! If I were to make a list of your qualities and attributes, it would need to be a mile long. Maybe even more.

But there are no maybes about this: you're the kind of person the world needs more of. I wish I could wave a magic wand and give everyone more of your understanding and insight, more of your loving kindness, more of your joy, and more of all the special things I see in you time and time again.

You're one of my favorite people ever, and my days are always sweeter, easier, and infinitely more blessed when you are in them.

*I think I know what your superpower is.
It's making people happy.*

You are so considerate and caring. Being around you lifts up my spirits and always makes me feel more at peace. So many of the personal qualities I aspire to... are the ones I see in you.

I love your sweet nature, your sage advice, your delightful sense of humor, and all the ways you encourage so many brighter days to come around. And I know for a fact that everyone who knows you feels the same way I do. You touch so many lives with your joy and thoughtfulness.

You really are — and you always will be — just the best.

When You Need a Little More Sunshine in Your Life, I Want You to Remember This...

You are in my heart today... and very much on my mind.

When you have a quiet moment, I want you to imagine me here... smiling the way I always do when I think of you. I hope you know that so many prayers and wishes are in those smiles.

My prayers are for you to have strength, encouragement, and so much to look forward to.

My wishes are for you to know how much you're cared about.

My heart wants you to be blessed with so much serenity.

And I hope you know how often my thoughts… are all for you.

Twenty Beautiful Things That Are True About You

You are something — and someone — very special. You really are. No one else in this entire world is exactly like you. You're a one-of-a-kind treasure, uniquely here in this space and time.

You are here to shine in your own wonderful way, sharing your smile in the best way you can and remembering all the while that a little light somewhere makes a brighter light everywhere.

You can — and you do — make a generous contribution to this world, and there are so many beautiful things about you.

You have qualities within you that many people would love to have, and those who really and truly know you are so glad that they do…

You have a big heart and a good and sensitive soul. You are gifted with thoughts and ways of seeing things that only special people know. You know that life doesn't always play by the rules but that, in the long run, everything will work out. You understand that you and your actions are capable of turning anything around — and that joys once lost can always be found.

There is a resolve and an inner reserve of strength in you that few ever get to see. You have so many treasures within — those you're only beginning to discover... and all the ones you're already aware of.

Never forget what a treasure you are. That special person in the mirror may not always get to hear all the compliments you so sweetly deserve, but you are so worthy of such an abundance
...of friendship, joy,
and love.

Every Day
Should Have a Wish List
(Here Is Mine for You)

I Wish You...

A thankful heart. *Filled with friendship
   and love.
Memories. You'll treasure forever.
Faith and courage. To rise above.
And reminders. Of how special you are.*

*Joy. To give you twinkles in your eyes.
Blessings. From angels in disguise.
Health and hope. On this
   journey through life.
And the very best. Of everything!*

Just Between Us

If it weren't for you, I wouldn't have half
as much laughter or nearly as much joy.

I wouldn't have as much peace or
understanding. And I definitely wouldn't
have as much fun!

I love that you're here. And whether it's in person or on the phone... I love the connection that is always there between us.

What we share is really something special. I feel more at home with you than I do with just about anyone, and feelings like those are some of the most precious of all.

I will always be filled with gratitude... for so many things about you.

It just comes so naturally to you to share your goodness and kindness with everyone around you. I think you were born with a smile in your heart, and it's one you share so openly. My days are always better when you're in them.

Whenever my heart is overflowing with pleasant thoughts and peaceful feelings, I always know it's because I've been thinking of you. And I just want you to know...

*One of the things I love most about my
life... is having you in it.*

If you could see yourself reflected in my eyes, you would see someone who makes my heart just smile inside. You would catch a glimpse of somebody who has been such a terrific influence on me and who keeps on making a beautiful difference in my days.

*If you could hear the words I would love
to share, you would be able to listen to a
special tribute to you, one that sings your
praises and describes how much I'll always
cherish you.*

*If you could imagine one of the nicest gifts
anyone could ever receive, you would begin
to understand what your presence in my
life has meant to me.*

My Hopes
and Happy Wishes
for You

Lots more time to do the things you really love doing.
Much less time spent worrying about this and that.
Recognizing all you've accomplished and realizing
each day is a gift... waiting to be unwrapped.

Believing in yourself and being open to all the
good things that are going to come your way.
And truly, beautifully celebrating all that you are:
*   someone I care about more than I can say.*

*You are so important to my days...
and so essential to the smile
    within me.
That certain space where our lives
overlap is the place that brings me
the most understanding,
    the most peace,
the nicest memories, and a joy that
    comes to my heart so constantly.*

*And I want you to know that
I wouldn't trade the days
    I've spent with you for anything.*

Well… maybe just one thing.

A million more just like them.

You Are All Kinds of Awesome

With arms that are wide open and a heart that is so full, I just want to say... thank you, thank you, thank you.

You're a one-of-a-kind wonder, a beautiful reflection of all the kindness in your heart, and a special gift to the world.

I'm really glad to have this chance to let you know how I feel and to shine a little light on your wonderfulness.

A Little Story About "You and Me"

Me: So lucky to have this special connection!
You: The special person I'm so thankful for.

Me: Someone who means well, but doesn't always get it right.
You: Someone who gives my life so many smiles and so much encouragement.

Me: A little insecure, a little uncertain, a little crazy sometimes.
You: A huge help and a calming influence... all the time.

You: *Know what's going on inside me better than anyone.*

Me: *There isn't anybody else I can trust like this and no one I feel so comfortable turning to.*

You: *On a scale of 1 to 10, with 10 being the best, at least a 20.*

Me: *Counting my blessings and hearing your name come up so many times.*

You: *A joy to be with, to think of, and just to talk to.*

Me: *So incredibly glad… there's you.*

It seems like I'm always searching for a way to tell you how marvelous I think you are.

And I thought that maybe these words could help me convey a few thoughts that I would love to share with you...

You're my definition of a special person.

I think you're fantastic.
And exceptional and unique and endearing.
To me, you're someone
who is very necessary to my well-being.
In so many ways, you fill my life
with happiness and the sweet feelings
of being so grateful that you're here.

I could go on and on…
*   but you get the picture.*

I think you're a masterpiece.

Such a Blessing

In the course of a person's lifetime, there are so many prayers that get whispered and so many hopes that fill the heart. There are wishing stars that spend their entire evenings listening to all the things we long for.

I have said those prayers and had those hopes and chatted with more than my share of stars in the sky.

*I always feel that if I ask and believe and wish
well enough, some things are bound to turn
out right.*

*But in all my prayers and wishes and hopes,
I couldn't have asked for
    a blessing
        more beautiful
            than you in my life.*

For You

I don't know exactly what it is… but there is something very special about you.

It might be all the things I see on the surface: Things that everyone notices and admires about you. Qualities and capabilities. Your easygoing smile, obviously connected to a warm and loving heart. It might be all the things that set you apart from everyone else…

Maybe it's the big things: The way you never hesitate to go a million miles out of your way to do what's right. The way your todays help set the stage for so many beautiful tomorrows. Or maybe it's the little things: Words shared heart to heart. An unspoken understanding. Sharing seasons. Making some very lovely memories. The joys of two people just being on the same page in each other's history.

If I could ever figure out all the magic that makes you so special, I'd probably find out that it's a combination of all these things — blended together with the best this world has to offer...

Friendship and love, dreams come true, strong feelings, gentle talks, listening, laughing, and simply knowing someone whose light shines brighter than any star.

You really are amazing.

And I feel very lucky to have been given the gift of knowing how special you are.

I'm Going to Be Here for You, No Matter What

When you need someone to turn to, I'll be here for you. I will do whatever it takes and give as much as I can... to help you find your smile and get you back on steady ground again.

When you just need to talk, I will listen with my heart. And I will do my best to hear the things you may want to say but can't quite find the words for.

I will never betray the trust you put in me. All I will do is keep on caring and doing my best to see you through...

If there are decisions to be made, I may offer a direction to go in. If there are tears to be dried, I will tenderly dry them.

I want you to feel completely at ease about reaching out to me.

And don't ever forget this: you couldn't impose on me if you tried. It simply isn't possible.

Your happiness and peace of mind are so closely interwoven with mine that they are inseparable.

I will truly, deeply, and completely care about you every day. You can count on that.

I hope it will invite a little more serenity into your life to know you're not alone.

And I hope it will encourage a brighter day to shine through.

I'm not going anywhere. I promise.

Unless it's to come to your side and to hold out a hand... to you.

A Gentle Reminder of What a Joy It Is to Have You in My Life!

You are always with me,
   here in my heart.

Your goodness is such a gift.
Everywhere your journey takes you…
   you spread so much happiness.
You have a truly lovable spirit
   and a kind and caring soul.

You are a very special person.
You are a joy to know.

I Don't Know What I'd Do Without You

To you:

For keeping my spirits up.
For never letting me down.
For being here for me.
For knowing I'm there for you.

For bringing so many smiles my way.
For being sensitive to my needs.
For knowing just what to say.
For listening better than anyone else.

For bringing me laughter.
For bringing me light.
For understanding so much about me.
For trusting me with so much about you.

For being the best.
For being so beautiful.

I don't know what I'd do
...without you.

For the Times When You Need a Hug, I Want You to Remember This...

I know you have those days, just like I do, when the quiet, kind warmth of a hug would make everything better.

Hugs are such reassuring things. They remind us that we're not alone. That somebody cares. They let us know we have a connection to another person... someone special... who can wrap their arms around us and make us feel like we're understood and wished so many good things.

That's what I want these words to bring to you.

Every time you need a hug and I'm not there to give it, I want you to hold on to the words in this book and let them hug you back.

Special People

The special people in this world are the most precious people of all. No matter what happens, they always understand. They never hesitate to go out of their way. They hold your hand.

They bring you smiles when a smile is exactly what you need. They listen, and they hear what is said in the spaces between the words.

*They care, and they let you know you're in
their prayers.*

*Special people always know the perfect thing
to do. They can make your whole day just by
saying something that no one else could have
said. Sometimes you feel like they share with
you a secret language that others can't tune in
to. They can guide you, comfort you, and light
up your life with laughter...*

Special people understand your moods and nurture your needs, and they lovingly know just what you're after.

When your feelings come from deep inside and they need to be spoken to someone you don't have to hide from, you share them... with special people. When good news comes, special people are the first ones you turn to. And when feelings overflow and tears need to fall, special people help you through it all.

Special people bring sunlight into your life. They warm your world whether they are far away or close by your side.

Special people are gifts
that bring such happiness
and they're treasures
that money can't buy.

Thoughts for You

One of the most tender places in my heart
   will always be saved for you.
You...
      the one person I can always talk to;
      the one person who understands.
You...
      for making me laugh in the rain;
      for helping me shoulder my troubles.

You...
   for loving me in spite of myself
   and always putting me
      back on my feet again.
You...
   for giving me someone to believe in;
   someone who lets me know that
   there really is goodness and kindness
   and laughter and love in the world.
You...
   for being one of the best
   parts of my life and proving it
      over and over again.

Twenty~Four Things to Always Remember... and One Thing to Never Forget

Your presence is a present to the world.
You're unique and one of a kind.
Your life can be what you want it to be.
Take the days just one at a time...

Count your blessings, not your troubles.
You'll make it through whatever comes along.
Within you are so many answers.
Understand, have courage, be strong.

Don't put limits on yourself.
So many dreams are waiting to be realized.

Decisions are too important to leave to chance.
Reach for your peak, your goal, your prize.

Nothing wastes more energy than worrying.
The longer one carries a problem,
    the heavier it gets.
Don't take things too seriously.
Live a life of serenity, not a life of regrets...

Remember that a little love goes a long way.
Remember that a lot... goes forever.
Remember that friendship is a wise investment.
Life's treasures are people... together.

Realize that it's never too late.
Do ordinary things in an extraordinary way.
Have health and hope and happiness.
Take the time to wish upon a star.

And don't ever forget…
for even a day…
    how very special you are.

What It Takes

It takes a certain kind of person to be special.

It takes someone who is really remarkable; someone who lights up this little corner of the world with feelings of friendship and love and understanding. It takes a truly unique personality and a knack for making life happier and more rewarding.

*It takes someone who's willing to
take the time. It takes an individual
who is able to open up and share their
innermost feelings with another. It
takes someone who makes the path
of life an easier and more satisfying
journey. It takes a rare combination of
many qualities.*

*It takes a certain kind of person
to be special.*

*It takes someone
...exactly like you.*

I cherish that you understand me so well and that I know you just about as well as I could ever know anyone.

*I am blessed by the countless smiles
we have shared, by the laughter that
lingers in my heart, and by our concerns
that have found a place of comfort in
the sanctuary of our caring. I truly
don't know what I'd do... without the
goodness you give my life.*

I Wish for You

Happiness. Deep down within.

Serenity. With each sunrise.

Success. In each facet of your life.

Close and caring friends.

Love. That never ends.

Special memories. Of all the yesterdays.

A bright today. With so much to be thankful for.

A path. That leads to beautiful tomorrows.

Dreams. That do their best to come true.

And a real understanding. Of all the adorable things about you.

Every Time I Think of You, My Heart Overflows with Gratitude

You're someone I think about so much…
and somebody I think the world of.

I have benefited so much by your presence in
my life… and by all the things you do and
give and share. My days are always better
because of you, and I'm always happier and
more at peace when you're in my thoughts.

I care about you so much, and I always will.
The positive spirit you bring to everything
and everyone around you is really
something special and precious and rare.

You are a breath of fresh air in the lives of so many people, and you deserve a huge amount of gratitude for all that you do.

I want to say this a thousand times over and with all my heart: thank you.

Here Are My Most Grateful Feelings for You... All Summed Up in One Very Special Note

Don't ask me how I know this... I just do.

I know that there is no one else in the world like you. You are such a beautiful human being, and I am so glad for every treasured thing you are to me. Everyone should have a shining light in their life, and I've thanked my lucky stars a million times... that I have you.

You understand so much, so well, so naturally. I think people with big hearts are just that way... but your heart seems to me like the most caring one of all.

I love so many things about you, and I will forever be indebted for the way you make everything better.

When you look at me, I know you see someone who is far from perfect. But you have this angel way of taking the good... and making me feel great about it. You take the bad... and you help me feel okay about it. When you notice that there's something I'm struggling with... you know just what to say to encourage me on. And when the two things I need most are acceptance and hope, those are invaluable gifts you instinctively know how to give...

So… I want to give this to you. I want to say that you're enormously appreciated and simply the best. You're someone I'll always be thankful for and somebody I feel very blessed to know.

Although this book is now coming to a close, I want its messages to stay in your heart endlessly.

And I hope you'll
        always remember…
                how special you are
                        to me.

About the Author

Best-selling author and editor Douglas Pagels has inspired millions of readers with his insights and his anthologies. His books have sold over 3 million copies, and he is one of the most quoted contemporary writers on the Internet today. Reflecting a philosophy that is perfect for our times, Doug has a wonderful  knack for sharing his thoughts and sentiments in a voice that is so positive and understanding we can't help but take the message to heart.

His writings have been translated into over a dozen languages due to their global appeal and inspiring outlook on life, and his work has been quoted by many worthy causes and charitable organizations.

He and his wife live in Colorado, and they are both parents and grandparents. Over the years, Doug has spent much of his time as a classroom volunteer, a youth basketball coach, an advocate for local environmental issues, a frequent traveler, and a craftsman, building a cabin in the Rocky Mountains.